THE Bliss LIST

JOURNAL

Companion to *The Bliss List*

THE B1ISS LIST

JOURNAL

Companion to *The Bliss List*

J.P. HANSEN

CAREER BLISS PUBLICATIONS
OMAHA, NE

ISBN10: 0-9840934-2-7
ISBN13: 978-0-9840934-2-7
Publisher Cataloging in Publication Data

Career Bliss Publications, Inc.
13518 L St.
Omaha, Nebraska 68137
www.YourBlissList.com

Book Design: Gary James Withrow
Production, Distribution, and Marketing: Concierge Marketing Inc.

Printed in the United States of America

10 9 8 7 6 5 4 3 2 1

Introduction

Congratulations on your purchase of *The Bliss List Journal*. This is meant to accompany *The Bliss List* (if you need a copy, they are available at www.YourBlissList.com). This workbook will help you maximize the power of *The Bliss List*. Consider this book to be your working diary—your personal guide to living the dream at work (and life). You will have ample space to write your thoughts and create action plans with *The Bliss List*. Before you begin reading *The Bliss List*, start with the following assessment, titled "Gratitude and Grievances."

Get ready to *be* your bliss!

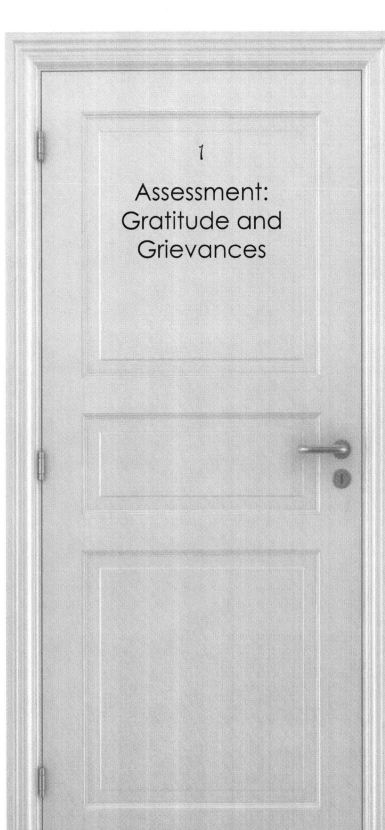

1

Assessment: Gratitude and Grievances

"Gratitude helps you to grow and expand; gratitude brings joy and laughter into your life and into the lives of all those around you."
—Eileen Caddy

Let's Clear the Air!

For this lesson, let's clear the air right off the bat. I'll give you some space to list all your grievances you have about your current job, boss, company or life. Write for as long as you feel you need to—take as much time as you want; air it all out:

Grievances: _____

_____

_____

_____

_____

_____

_____

_____

Finished? Look over what you just wrote. As you re-read it, notice how you feel? Does it make you feel angry? Depressed? Hateful? Scorned? However you felt, it probably wasn't good. If you are like most people, you probably felt bad. Real bad—lousy even!

Gratitude

Now, we'll reverse the exercise and title it "Gratitude." Start writing the things you are grateful for with your current job. It may take a little time, but write the first things that pop in your mind, no matter how trivial they may seem. Write for as long as you want:

I am grateful for: _____

_____

_____

_____

_____

_____

_____

_____

_____

_____

_____

After you finish, look it over. As you re-read it, again notice how you feel? Are you in better spirits? You should be. Hopefully, you felt happy as you wrote and re-read it.

"Gratitude bestows reverence,
allowing us to encounter everyday epiphanies,
those transcendent moments of awe that change forever
how we experience life and the world."
—John Milton

This is a very important exercise in getting you prepared for attracting your dream job—for how you encounter true epiphanies. For the next five days, take five minutes and do this simple gratitude exercise. Don't worry if there is overlap. You may write the same things; it doesn't matter if you do or don't. Just focus on what you are grateful for. Mark this page so you can easily return to it, and do this first thing in the morning:

Day 1 Gratitude: ....
....
....
....

Day 2 Gratitude: ....
....
....
....

Day 3 Gratitude: ....
....
....
....

Day 4 Gratitude: ....

....

....

....

Day 5 Gratitude: ....

....

....

....

After five days, re-read each passage that you wrote. Notice how you feel while reading each word or phrase. You probably felt good.

Now it's decision time. If, after five days of doing this exercise, you have had a change of heart—you feel that your job is better than you originally thought, this is a good thing. Think of how you could enhance your current job to make it even better; in this case, you may be able to start seeing it as more of a dream job. It may mean writing down what is truly missing: money, bonus potential, feeling more important, etc., and then setting an action plan to obtain the missing element(s). If this is the case, great. Read on.

If, after five days, you still want out of your current job, don't fret: at least you tried. It's time to focus your energy on getting that dream job.

2

Find Your Bliss

*"Nothing is more important
than reconnecting with your bliss.
Nothing is as rich.
Nothing is more real."*
—Deepak Chopra

B y now, you have hopefully started reading *The Bliss List* (available at www.YourBlissList.com). For this important exercise, simply write down what makes you feel the happiest. It doesn't have to be work-related. What makes time stand still for you? This is your Bliss List. Is it living like a millionaire? Being your own boss? The security of a stable company? Skimming over a lake in a sailboat? Skiing down a mountain? Hiking in the wilderness? Reading a spellbinding book? You decide.

This list should come naturally to you and not take more than a few minutes for you to write. You actually will feel your mood improve as you think about, and write, this list. Whatever you write, the only rule is that you tell yourself what makes you happy—not what makes your spouse, family, boss, friends, clergy, or whoever happy. Don't place any limits on yourself.

This list is your Bliss List. Write at least fifteen words and phrases now:

My Bliss List

1. _____

_____

_____

_____

2. _____

_____

_____

_____

3. _____

_____

_____

_____

4. _____

_____

_____

_____

5. _____

_____

_____

_____

6.

7.

8.

9.

10.

11.

12. _____

13. _____

14. _____

15. _____

Does your list have a degree of challenge in it? I hope so. Remember, your list has no boundaries or limits. The higher you set your goals, the greater your results. Don't short yourself on your Bliss List; challenge yourself. Try it one more time with more challenge:

My New Bliss List

1.

2.

3.

4.

5.

6. _____
_____
_____
_____

7. _____
_____
_____
_____

8. _____
_____
_____
_____

9. _____
_____
_____
_____

10. _____
_____
_____
_____

11. _____
_____
_____
_____

12. _____

_____

_____

_____

13. _____

_____

_____

14. _____

_____

_____

15. _____

_____

_____

Now that you have completed and revised your top fifteen, we'll cut it down to a top seven. It has been scientifically proven that the human brain is capable of handling only seven things at once. To pare your list, simply compare and rank your 1 vs. 2, and then 1 vs. 3, then 1 vs. 4, and so on down the list. Whatever comes out on top at the end will comprise your Top Seven Bliss List—your primary goals:

Top Seven Bliss List

1. ....

2. ....

3. ....

4. ....

5. ....

6. ....

7. ....

This Top Seven Bliss List is you. Use another piece of paper to write down your Top Seven Bliss List. Post this list in plain sight and put one in your wallet or purse too. The more concentrated thought you place against this list with enthusiastic feeling and confidence, the quicker all seven will manifest in your life. I want you to go seven for seven here.

Now, we're going to apply your Top Seven into a first draft for your ideal job. You may have more than one ideal job: the more, the better (no limits, remember?). Write the title or titles of your dream job or jobs—even if the title is fictitious It doesn't matter. Under each title, write a brief description of what this job entails. Intersperse your Top Seven into it—they should be a match. Remember, don't limit yourself to only salary. Think of what really makes you happy. The money will follow:

Dream Job Title: _____
    Dream Job Description: _____

_____

_____

_____

_____

Dream Job Title: _____
    Dream Job Description: _____

_____

_____

_____

_____

Dream Job Title: _____

    Dream Job Description: _____

_____

_____

_____

Next, write down what skills are necessary to do this job; under this, write the skills you already possess. How does it match up? It probably is not too far off:

Dream Job Title: _____

_____

_____

_____

Skills I Have: _____

_____

_____

_____

What additional steps are needed? If more education is required, list it. Will you need additional credentials like a certification? Would a degree or an additional class or a training seminar or merely a different company environment help you to obtain what is missing? Be honest and take no shortcuts. This is your dream job:

Necessary Steps Needed: _____

_____

_____

_____

Bliss Cards

It's time to start amplifying your desires. The more you think of something with enthusiasm and confidence, the more likely you are to manifest your goals in your life.

For this exercise, you simply need some 3-x 5-inch cards. These will be your Bliss Cards. Write your Top Seven Bliss List items on a card and keep it with you wherever you go: in your wallet/purse, pocket, dashboard of your car, on your refrigerator, and in your briefcase. Keep your list in a strategic place where you are most apt to view it often during the day. It is a very powerful tool in turning your Bliss List into reality.

After you have achieved one of the items on your Bliss List, make a new one and save your card in a folder labeled "Bliss List Successes."

Also, your Bliss List may change; you actually want it to change—and to grow. Remember, you are energy and are always moving. You will evolve, and so will your list. Update it every three months or as needed.

I know you may be a little skeptical. What do you have to lose?

(Keep a record on these pages of your Bliss Cards)

Bliss Card #1   Date:_____

_____

_____

_____

_____

Bliss Card #1 Success   Date:_____

_____

_____

_____

_____

Bliss Card #2   Date:_____

_____

_____

_____

_____

Bliss Card #2 Success   Date:_____

_____

_____

_____

_____

Bliss Card #3   Date:_____

_____

_____

_____

_____

Bliss Card #3 Success   Date:_____

_____

_____

_____

_____

Bliss Card #4   Date:_____

_____

_____

_____

_____

Bliss Card #4 Success   Date:_____

_____

_____
_____
_____

Bliss Card #5   Date:_____

_____

_____
_____
_____

Bliss Card #5 Success   Date:_____

_____

_____
_____
_____

Bliss Card #6   Date:_____

_____

_____
_____
_____

Bliss Card #6 Success   Date:_____

_____

_____
_____
_____

Send in your success stories to www.YourBlissList.com
(Be part of the sequel!)

Your Bliss Board

The more intensity you give to your thoughts, the stronger they become. Your attention to your goals allows them to manifest more quickly in your life. A powerful tool to help you strengthen your thoughts and vibration—and to help you obtain your bliss more quickly—is to use a Bliss Board.

As the name implies, basically it is like a bulletin board. It is comprised of your goals and desires. Vivid, colorful pictures are ideal and very powerful. Fill your Bliss Board with the top phrases that describe what makes you happy. Whatever you desire and think about with enthusiasm and confidence will manifest itself.

You can have more than one Bliss Board. I keep at least three Bliss Boards in my office, along with framed affirmations such as these: "Money Comes Easily and Frequently," "Every Day, in Every Way, I am Getting Better, Better, and Better," "Negative Thoughts, Negative Suggestions, Have No Influence over Me at Any Level of Mind," and "Desire, Believe, Expect, and Be Grateful."

The trick is to keep your mind laser-focused on what you truly want. Meditating and visualizing your Bliss Boards and affirmations also magnifies your vibration tremendously. The more you can intensify your goals, the more likely you will obtain them.

Be creative with your Bliss Board. Have fun with it. The more realistic you can make it—using pictures in 3D and colors that appeal to you—the more effective it will be. Cut out pictures from magazines or print colored images from the Internet. Place your Bliss Board in a prominent location where you will see it often.

I keep my three Bliss Boards at eye level right around my computer screen, and every time I look at them (and it is often), I always try to feel as though my goals and desires are in the present—as if I already have them.

What is on my three Bliss Boards? My first is simply for "Harmonic Wealth: Financial, Relational, Intellectual, Physical, and Spiritual." My second Bliss Board pertains to this book: "#1 Bestseller, Help More Than 100,000 People, Financial Independence, Abundant Prosperity, and an Oprah appearance." My third is a copy of the cover page for this book. Since you are one of the 100,000 who bought this book and are actually reading it, I am one step closer to one of my goals. I am grateful for you.

Do a Bliss Board. It only takes a few minutes to do. You already have a Top Seven Bliss List, so it should be easy—and fun. The results will amaze you.

You can order your high quality authorized Bliss Board
and accessories at www.YourBlissList.com.

Your Bliss Jar

Take a jar (Bliss Jars are available at www.YourBlissList.com) and tape a note on top of the jar stating, "Whatever is contained in this Bliss Jar—IS!" Write each goal individually on a small piece of paper, then reread it with enthusiastic feeling, and simply drop each one into the jar. You will be amazed at how many of your little notes actually come true.

Now, write your blissful dream job and be as specific as you can and reread it; then drop it into your jar.

Every single goal I have deposited into my Bliss Jar has miraculously come true. Bliss Jars make miracles seem common. It takes only a few minutes, but the results will astound you (at first).

To get started, you may want to use the fifteen items you listed in your original Bliss List. Though you pared the list down to seven so you wouldn't overload your brain, capable of handling only seven things at once, you cannot overload your Bliss Jar. There are no limits. Write all fifteen goals down separately and drop 'em into the jar. It will start working its magic right after you close the lid on the jar.

The first time something you wrote comes true—and it will—start a new jar. Label it your "Gratitude Jar" and pop each item as it comes true into the new jar. This will serve as a constant reminder of your gratitude and the fact that your Bliss Jar works.

The more you can formalize your thoughts, the more likely your goals will manifest. Bliss Lists, Cards, Boards, and Jars all help bring your desires into reality.

Please send in your success stories with your Bliss Jar to
www.YourBlissList.com.

3

Opening
New Doors
to Your Bliss

Opening New Doors
to Your Bliss

y now you know how important it is to write down your goals and aspirations. Here's the perfect place for you to record your thoughts from day to day to help get you in the habit of doing it.

Top Seven Bliss List

Date:

1. _____
_____
_____
_____

2. _____
_____
_____
_____

3. _____
_____
_____
_____

4. _____
_____
_____
_____

5. _____
_____
_____
_____

6.

7.

Top Seven Bliss List

Date:

1. _____
_____
_____
_____

2. _____
_____
_____
_____

3. _____
_____
_____
_____

4. _____
_____
_____

5. _____
_____
_____
_____

6.

7.

Dream Job #1

Dream Job Title: _____

    Dream Job Description: _____

_____

_____

_____

Next, write down what skills are necessary to do this job; under this, write the skills you already possess. How does it match up? It probably is not too far off:

Necessary Skills: _____

_____

_____

_____

Skills I Have: _____

_____

_____

_____

What steps are needed? If more education is required, list it. Will you need additional education/credentials like a certification? Would a degree or an additional class or a training seminar or merely a different company environment help you to obtain what is missing? Be honest and no shortcuts.

Dream Job #2

Dream Job Title: _____

Dream Job Description: _____

_____

_____

_____

Next, write down what skills are necessary to do this job. Again, write the skills you already possess. How does this one match up?

Necessary Skills: _____

_____

_____

_____

Skills I Have: _____

_____

_____

_____

What steps are needed? If more education is required, list it. Will you need additional education/credentials like a certification? Would a degree or an additional class or a training seminar or merely a different company environment help you to obtain what is missing? Be honest and no shortcuts.

On this date, _____ my goal is: _____

_____

_____

On this date, _____ my goal is: _____

_____

_____

On this date, _____ my goal is: _____

_____

_____

On this date, _____ I want: _____

_____

_____

4

The Six Spokes
of Bliss

Spiritual   Relational

THE 6 SPOKES OF

Physical   Financial

Emotional   Intellectual

T hink of yourself as a wheel with six spokes. To work at your optimum level, each spoke needs to be as strong as possible. I want you to go six for six. Go easy on yourself if a couple of your spokes are rusty or even broken. We all know someone who may possess one spoke that is out of sync. For example, in the financial spoke; there are plenty of billionaires who are spiritually, physically, and emotionally bankrupt (I'm not naming names, since they can afford better lawyers than me).

Does your Bliss List include all six? If not, go back and revise.

I'll give you some space to formulate goals for each key spoke:

Spiritual:

_____

_____

_____

_____

_____

_____

_____

_____

_____

Relational:

_____

_____

_____

_____

_____

_____

_____

_____

_____

Intellectual: _____

_____

_____

_____

_____

_____

_____

_____

_____

_____

Emotional: _____

_____

_____

_____

_____

_____

_____

_____

_____

_____

Physical:

_____

_____

_____

_____

_____

_____

_____

_____

_____

_____

Financial:

_____

_____

_____

_____

_____

_____

_____

_____

_____

_____

5

Goals Just
Around
the Corner

Goals Just Around
the Corner

N ow is the time to put on paper all of those tasks and goals that are always lingering at the back of your mind – those things you lie in bed at night thinking about. If you've been paying any attention, you'll know by now that actually writing them down will greatly increase your chances of accomplishing them.

Immediate Personal Goals

Books I want to read for personal enjoyment

Tasks I want to get done around the house

How I plan to stay in shape and be healthy

Other items

Things to Accomplish
in Other Areas of My Life

Add updated items to my résumé _____

_____

_____

_____

_____

_____

_____

_____

_____

Groups I will join or monitor for networking _____

_____

_____

_____

_____

_____

_____

_____

_____

_____

Skills I want to learn

_____

_____

_____

_____

_____

_____

_____

_____

_____

_____

_____

Places to which I want to travel

_____

_____

_____

_____

_____

_____

_____

_____

_____

_____

_____

_____

_____

Other items

Career Goals

1 year goals

3 year goals

5 year goals

Lifetime goals

6

Writing a Killer Résumé, Your Invisible First Impression

Writing a Killer Résumé,
Your Invisible First Impression

I want you to re-read this section. It's that important. Afterwards, I'll give you a template where you can write your résumé using our tested approach.

Remember your decision about your first job? You spent a mere few hours or even minutes determining where you were going to spend the bulk of your waking time. Scary. Here's something even more scary. You'll spend even less time on one of the most important means for you to obtain your blissful dream job—your résumé.

You know the importance of a good first impression. Yet very few people spend enough time on their true first impression—their résumés. Believe me, I've seen plenty of lousy résumés—some I'll share soon. These people didn't think of their résumé as their first impression. This mindset (a real hindrance) will only keep them stuck in the mud and certainly not propel them into a blissful dream job.

Your résumé is your invisible first impression. And it goes without saying how important first impressions are.

The One-Page Myth

I had an executive level manager—we'll call him Jim—argue with me trying to defend his single-page (and inadequate) résumé. After college, he had worked for three blue-chip companies. He had a consistent track record of achievement and the promotions to show for it, accounting for a total of seven jobs in fourteen years of professional experience. Impressive background—and perfect for the job I was hoping to place him in.

Jim should have been a no-brainer for the Vice President job my firm was retained to fill. He had all the qualifications and then some—but they were not on paper (first impression). In my opinion, Jim had short-changed his career by shoe-horning it into only one page.

The result: I presented his résumé to my client whose first words were, "Looks light." (No kidding!)

Sometimes, that's all it takes to derail your opportunity to interview and lose a potential dream job. Since this particular client was a personal friend of many years, I attempted to push back with, "Oh, it's only a résumé. You will really like this guy!" I didn't sound too convincing.

"Who else do you have?" he replied with a disturbed tone.

There wasn't much more I could do except to slide Jim in with other candidates—later. I knew if I could just get him in front of the hiring manager, he would nail it—in spite of his lame résumé. This entire dilemma was due to his wimpy, one-page résumé—creating a poor first impression.

Unless you spend the time necessary to give yourself a positive first impression with an attention-grabbing résumé that rocks (I'll help make the process easier than you think), you may as well resign yourself to the fact that you'll never be given the opportunity. On my wall, I have a saying, "Success means being ready when opportunity knocks."

Having the best résumé you possibly can is being ready for that opportunity and will lead you to success.

I'm frequently asked, "What is the best résumé format?" You could ask ten people this question and may very well get ten different answers. The best résumé is one that moves yours to the top of the pile with the hiring manager. How? After years of trial and error, I have formulated an ideal résumé format that works. First, I'll describe it and then later give you some examples and a template.

The best résumé covers two areas: (1) activities and (2) accomplishments in chronological order, beginning with your most recent job. Use sentences in paragraph form for the activities and bullet points to highlight your accomplishments.

Some résumé advisers say you should do your résumé in the form of a letter. My answer: if that's what your dream company wants, that's what you do, but the most widely accepted résumé is still done chronologically by job/company.

Many times, a recruiter may do his or her own "write up" about you in lieu of your résumé. Make it easy by having a strong chronological résumé with clear descriptions of what you do/did and what you accomplished. This should give a recruiter enough ammo to present your qualifications with enthusiasm.

Ready to begin? First off, don't feel as if you have to pay a résumé service to do your résumé for you. Résumé services tend to follow templates that lack individuality. Don't defer your dream job quest to an outside service. Write it yourself. Use Microsoft® Word if you have it. Word is the most accepted business software. Chances are, a résumé service would type it on Word anyway. As another bonus, doing it yourself gives you the very important option of altering and tailoring your content to fit your target dream companies.

When listing your name at the top of the first page, use your nickname (the name you go by) rather than your full legal name. This adds a little warmth to the start and helps you avoid having to ask the hiring manager to call you something else right off the bat (first impressions). There's a big difference in listing Daniel Arthur Worthington, III vs. Dan Worthington.

Paragraph Your Activities

This is the mundane but necessary part of your résumé.

In the first line, describe your primary, overall responsibility. What geography you cover, how many employees you manage, any clients you are directly responsible for, and anything that may be pertinent to companies you are targeting. For example: *Responsible for $100 million in annual sales in the eastern United States for a 550-item pet food manufacturer.*

Next, describe your company's reporting and operational structure. *Report to the Vice President of Sales, oversee a direct sales force at headquarters and a brokerage force at retail. Supervise 100 employees through eight direct reports: five Region Managers, two Divisional Category Managers and one Administrative Assistant.*

If you are directly responsible for any customers, especially large, recognizable ones, indicate them by name.

If you were able to obtain a position description for your target job, include anything that pertains to what the company is looking for in your background. Interject any applicable responsibilities accordingly. For example, if company X is looking for a people manager, include how many employees you manage and list their titles.

Do not fill your paragraph with flowery verbiage such as: *While keeping the company's best interests in mind.* Keep it clear and concise. Fewer syllables wins you points with the interviewer.

Bullet Point Your Accomplishments

Bullet points are the most important content and design element of your résumé. And, ironically, typically the format item most résumé writers forget to use. You actually learned about bullet points in your Advertising 101 class. Any time you can use objects in a presentation (a résumé is a presentation of you), the impact is far greater than merely with words. The reader is more likely to remember items highlighted with an object.

Your Advertising 101 class taught you that, ideally, you would use colored objects in a presentation, but, like the objects example, that's not sound advice for your résumé. Notwithstanding colored objects, bullet points are effective and easy to use (one click on the old toolbar). They draw the reader to your accomplishments. Using my bullet-point advice will catapult your résumé to the "must see" pile.

What do you want to bullet point? Accomplishments such as these:

- Increases in revenue
  (if double digit—more on this in a minute)
- Decreases in expenses
- Awards won
- Bonuses earned
- Rank vs. peers (especially if it's a #1)
- New innovative technique(s) designed by you
  and used by others
- Buzz words important to the target company
- Leadership/task forces, especially if chosen by
  senior management
- Teamwork
- Hiring, promoting employees
- Restructuring to improve efficiency

Bullet points must be believable yet impressive. How can you make them believable? Quantify and qualify—and without any passive words. Avoid using words such as implement, execute, or follow. The language in your bullet-pointed accomplishments should reflect strength and confidence. Use these strong words: created, designed, led, obtained, ranked #1, awarded, and so on. The following is a bullet-point example:

- Implemented sales programs

VERSUS

- Increased sales by 31.6% in FY 2008, +37.3% in FY 2007, and + 32.1% in FY 2006

Which bullet point is more effective? "Implemented sales programs" is too vague and is something anyone could say. It says, In short: it underwhelms the reader and sells you short.

The second bullet point quantifies (31.6%, 37.3%, and 32.1%) and qualifies (FY 2008, 2007, 2006). It is believable because of its precision and it is impressive—you always want to use double digits for increases.

What if you didn't have double digit increases? Well, you have to be creative. Not many employers say, "Get me some salespeople who can drive some stagnant, single-digit increases." Let's say your increases were a modest +3.2% in '08, +4.2% in '07 and +3.8% in '06. Your bullet point would be:

- Increased sales by 11.2% vs. industry average of +5.1%

I would advise you to leave out the three singular years and instead add them together, since you were in the job three years. And we added the "industry average" number, so the reader can see you more than doubled the industry average. It is still impressive and believable (quantified and qualified). Much more so than "Implemented sales programs."

Tailor your accomplishments to your target company's hot buttons. Place yourself in their shoes and brainstorm your most applicable successes. Be creative. List them in order of importance, with the top bullet point being the most important.

Which ones are the most important? The accomplishments most sought after by all companies are:

- Increasing revenues
- Decreasing expenses
- Increasing efficiencies

I'm going to repeat this point from earlier: quantify and qualify.

- Be specific.
- Avoid flowery verbiage.
- Use action verbs.

Be deliberate in marketing yourself. If you seek a position that will emphasize people development, list the number of employees you have developed and promoted.

Try to limit the number of bullet points to five for your most recent (and most important) position and three or fewer for earlier positions. Don't dilute your bullet points. Less is more here. Five impactful bullet points stand out and get the reader excited; eleven blend in and lose their impact, not to mention the reader.

The average time the interviewer will spend on your résumé is less than one minute. Less than one minute! Hit home runs with your bullet points. Ask your executive recruiter, "What is most important to the hiring manager?" and tailor your bullet points accordingly.

A candidate once told me—in trying to defend his weak résumé (and the fact that he was too lazy to re-do it)—that he didn't want to "give too much information on the résumé, or there wouldn't be anything to talk about in the interview." Wrong-O! A lousy résumé won't get you the interview. If properly written, though, a résumé can allow you to focus on chemistry with the interviewer versus explaining (that is, defending) your background. The following pages contain tips that will help your résumé shine.

NOTES:

Length

*"I didn't have time to write a short letter,
so I wrote a long one instead."*
-Mark Twain

If you follow the recommended chronological, paragraph, and bullet point format, your résumé should be as long as it needs to be. One-page résumés place you at a disadvantage, yet some people still believe a résumé should be one page (Procter & Gamble teaches this—probably so their employees don't get interviewed.). Twain's wisdom on letter writing is applicable to résumés, but don't short-change content for brevity's sake.

The one-pager is realistic for a recent college graduate; the more experience you have, the longer your résumé should be. If your résumé is clear, concise, and well-written, length should be a non-issue. So, length really doesn't matter (just wanted to see if you were still alert).

Contents

Sections entitled "Objectives" and "Career Summaries" are redundant and do not belong on a résumé. A well-written cover letter should serve as your career summary. The very fact that you are interested in this particular position means it is your objective.

Your résumé should include these headings:

Professional Experience
Education (all degrees—undergraduate and graduate, with grades listed if at least or higher than 3.0/4.0)
Honors (if applicable)
Professional Affiliations (if applicable)
Additional Training
Personal (optional)

If your target dream company is looking for a well-adjusted employee (usually defined in business circles as married with children), by all means, list it; if you're living in a van down by the river and are thrice divorced, do not include.

Some Résumé Don'ts

No picture of yourself (I've seen 'em) and no flowery verbiage. As a rule, if it can be stated with fewer words and syllables, do it. Think technical writing here. Don't use colored paper or cheap copier paper. Cotton-bound white paper is always a winner.

A confusing résumé, littered with typos will land you in the circular file. Fast. Take the time to proofread your résumé before it is printed! One of the best resources available is already in your computer—spell-check. Use it.

Don't think spell-check alone will suffice. You need to fine-tooth-comb your résumé, word for word. Years ago, even yours truly sent out 750 résumés to all of my targeted recruiting firms with the word manger. Guess what, spell-check let it go because manger is a word. But manger would have better described the nativity scene than the fact that I was a manager. Oops!

My eyes alone didn't catch this glaring typo. So, in addition to your careful proofreading, ask trusted colleagues and friends to critique your résumé for you. You only get one chance, and your first impression has to be perfect.

At the end of this book, in a section called Résumé Makeovers, I use some actual résumés from people with whom I have worked. I will show the "before" and "after" to help illustrate the differences between a résumé that will get placed in the round file (usually crumpled up) versus those moved to the top of the pile. Though the names have been altered, the basic content is verbatim.

NOTES:

Résumé Makeovers

Meet Barb. Barb was let go (out of the blue and with no warning) from a huge Fortune 100 pharmaceutical company. She hadn't kept up her résumé (understatement) and was in a bit of a panic when she called me. She was feeling pressure to obtain employment—and fast.

She's a well-paid sales executive, earning almost $200,000 in the most current year. Here is the original résumé she sent me. Does her résumé reflect that she is worth that much? I don't think so.

After speaking with Barb for about a half hour, I realized her résumé didn't reflect how well she was verbalizing her accomplishments either. This résumé, by her own admission, was "thrown together quickly." I asked, "Do you want "thrown together quickly" to keep you unemployed indefinitely?" Barb didn't laugh. I told her that it wouldn't take her very long to transform her résumé into something she was proud to use.

Her dilemma (and it wasn't a bad one to have): she had an interview lined up in three days for a great job—a different and more lucrative area of her industry with a well-respected company. She knew she had to work on her résumé—a lot. I gave her my tested résumé advice: "Use sentences in paragraph form to clearly describe the activities and bullet points to highlight what you accomplished." (Sound familiar? If not, you better turn back to chapter 3 and reread.)

Here's Barb's original, thrown-together résumé. The makeover follows.

BEFORE

BARB E. DAHL
31 South Main Street
Anytown, NJ 10012
609-200-0000 cellular
609-211-1111 home
bdahl@salesqueen.net

EMPLOYMENT:

6/04–8/08 **Pfeel Well Pay More, Inc.,**–Anytown,
NJ Senior Therapeutic Specialty Representative
Manage territory consisting of Anytown1/Anytown2: Methodist Hospital, All Well Health System, Anytown: St Elizabeth's Hospital, Bryant East and West, Freeme, Kowtown, and Havenot, New Jersey.
Call on specialty physicians i.e. general surgeons, orthopedic surgeons, neurologists, pain medicine, pulmonary/critical care, hospitalists, and emergency room physicians to increase product use and market share; develop and implement business plan, call cycle, and speaker activities within territory to insure coverage with respect to strategic capabilities; assist DM with training and mentoring two new representatives; support DM with setting up preceptorships and presenting POA topics.

7/02–6/04 **Slimmer Orthopedics**–Anytown, NJ
Territory Manager
Responsible for selling full line of orthopedic implants and trauma products to 9 hospitals and 2 surgery centers. In charge of negotiating prices for instruments, implants, and competitive conversions. Oversee use of Slimmer Orthopedics re-infusion products with spine and joint surgeons in Anytown. Present in surgery to support surgeons and staff in correct use of Slimmer Orthopedics instruments and implants. Conduct training session for surgical technicians and surgery staff on proper use of Slimmer equipment.

10/96–7/02 **Pfeel Well Pay More, Inc.,**–Anytown, NJ
Senior Institutional Healthcare Representative
Successfully sold all products in a variety of settings including:
Academic Medicine; University of New Jersey Medical Center, Clarkstein Hospital, Princeton University Medical Center
Federal Accounts; Anytown VAMC, Skyblue Air Force Base
Long Term Care; Ominouscare, Unicare, Kohlsteins
Managed Care; United Healthcare, Coventry, Blue Cross/Blue Shield
2001 IHR LAT MVP
Tryit Convention winner 1998
Zittec Convention winner 1998
Arthriticept Convention winner 1997
- 1998 VPC (#1 IHR in Region)
- 1998 Circle of Excellence (#6 in Division)
- 1998 IHR Rookie of the Year
- 1998 IHR Mover and Shaker Award winner (greatest change in GAR position)

7/89–10/96 **Wellfunded Financial**–Anytown, NJ
Compliance Auditor (10/95–10/96)
Oversee compliance functions of 28 consumer finance offices in eight Eastern States; perform compliance audits and cash integrity reviews and report findings to District

BEFORE

Managers and Executive Officers.

Branch Manager (7/89–10/95)
Manage and maintain $9 million finance office. Train and supervise staff of 7 in all aspects of daily business; approve and underwrite all lending and insurance decisions; set and oversee goals in order to meet employee and branch objectives; coordinate marketing plans for customers to accomplish branch goals; review all reports concerning trends and dealer activity to access areas of need or concern.

ORGANIZATIONS: International Credit Association
United Way Volunteer
Big Brothers/Big Sisters Volunteer

EDUCATION: **Perfect State College**–Perfect, NJ
Bachelor of Science, May 1989
Major: Business Administration/Marketing
Overall GPA: 3.55/4.0 **Major GPA:** 3.76/4.0
- Memorial Basketball Scholarship
- Perfect State College Basketball Scholarship -3 yr letter award
- Perfect State College Baseball Scholarship -3 yr letter award
- Rotary Club-Susie Dingbat Scholarship
- Academic Honors List
- Varsity Club President
- Phi Beta Landing Business Sorority

Did you notice she used sentence descriptions and bullet points for one of her jobs but not the other three? It was the first thing I noticed. And you can bet it would be the first thing the hiring manager would notice—just before she crumples it up and tosses it in the round file. You cannot use an inconsistent format on your résumé, whether you follow my advice or not.

The good news was that the toughest part of the résumé improvement process was over. She mentioned several outstanding accomplishments while we were talking, yet none of them were on her résumé. I told her all she had to do was to write what she had just told me.

Later the same day, Barb sent over this improved version:

AFTER

BARB E. DAHL
31 South Main Street
Anytown, NJ 10012
609-200-0000 cellular
bdahl@salesqueen.net

EMPLOYMENT:

Pfeel Good Pay More, Inc., –Anytown, NJ   6/04–Present

Senior Therapeutic Specialty Representative Anytown, NJ

Manage territory consisting of Anytown1/Anytown2: Methodist Hospital, All Well Health System, Anytown: St Elizabeth's Hospital, Bryant East and West, Freeme, Kowtown, and Havenot, New Jersey. Call on Specialty Physicians: General Surgeons, Orthopedic Surgeons, Neurologists, Pain Medicine, Pulmonary/Critical Care, Hospitalists, Endocrinologists, and Emergency Room Physicians to increase product use and market share; develop and implement business plan, call cycle, and speaker activities within territory to insure coverage with respect to strategic capabilities.

- Ranked #1 (out of 10) in District sales of Zittec–$2.3 million.
- Increased sales by 64% for Zittec over last year in #1 Zip Code, 10010–Anytown, NJ.
- Increased sales by 151% for Zittec over last year in #2 Zip Code, 10011, Beggan Mercy Medical Center.
- Increased Market Share of Zittec by 62.5%.
- Increased Market Share of Vfriend by 12.6% over last year.
- Currently at 110% of Zittec quota (#1 weighted product).
- Successfully launched 9 different drugs across 4 different medical specialties.

Slimmer Orthopedics–Warsaw, IN   7/02–6/04

Territory Manager—Anytown, NJ

Responsible for selling full line of orthopedic implants and trauma products to 9 hospitals and 2 surgery centers. In charge of negotiating prices for instruments, implants, and competitive conversions. Oversee use of Slimmer re-infusion products with spine and joint surgeons in Anytown. Present in surgery to support surgeons and staff in correct use of Slimmer instruments and implants. Conduct training session for surgical technicians and surgery staff on proper use of Slimmer equipment.

- Ranked #1 in class of 30 for Slimmer hip and knee training in Warsaw, IN.
- Successfully converted Faith Regional Hospital, Norfolk, NE to Slimmer trauma products. Successfully converted #1 Orthopedic Surgeon in Bohmfalk, NJ to Slimmer hip products—took volume from zero to $375,000 in first full year as Territory Manager.
- Increased territory volume from $560,000 to $980,000 in first full year as Territory Manager.

Pfeel Good Pay More, Inc., –Anytown, NJ   10/96–7/02

Senior Institutional Healthcare Representative–Anytown, NJ

Successfully sold all products in a variety of settings including: **Academic Medicine:** University of New Jersey Medical Center, Clarkstein Hospital, Princeton University Medical Center **Federal Accounts:** Anytown VAMC, Skyblue Air Force Base **Long Term Care:** Ominouscare, Unicare, Kohlsteins **Managed Care:** United Healthcare, Coventry, Blue Cross/Blue Shield.

- 2001 IHR LAT **MVP.**
- Tryit Convention winner 1998.
- Zittec Convention winner 1998.
- Arthriticept Convention winner 1997.
- 1998 VPC (#1 IHR in Region).
- 1998 Circle of Excellence.
- 1998 IHR **Rookie of the Year.**
- 1998 IHR **Mover and Shaker Award** winner (greatest change in GAR position).

AFTER

Wellfunded Financial–Anytown, NJ   07/89–10/96

Compliance Auditor   10/95–10/96

Oversee compliance functions of 28 consumer finance offices in eight Eastern States; perform compliance audits and cash integrity reviews and report findings to District Managers and Executive Officers.

Branch Manager   07/89–10/95

Manage and maintain $9 million finance office. Train and supervise staff of seven in all aspects of daily business; approve and underwrite all lending and insurance decisions; set and oversee goals in order to meet employee and branch objectives; coordinate marketing plans for customers to accomplish branch goals; review all reports concerning trends and dealer activity to access areas of need or concern.

ORGANIZATIONS:

United Way Volunteer, 2005–2006
Big Brothers/Big Sisters Volunteer, 2001–2003

ADDITIONAL TRAINING:

Pharmacology One
Pfeel Good Pay More Sales
Pfeel Good Pay More Institutional Selling IV
Pfeel Good Pay More Specialty Selling V
Targeted Selection
Associate Sales Director I
Evelyn Wood Speed Reading
"Converting to Yes" Pfeel Good Pay More Advanced Sales

EDUCATION:

Perfect State College–Perfect, NJ
Bachelor of Science, May 1989
Major: Business Administration/Marketing
Overall GPA: 3.55/4.0 **Major GPA:**3.76/4.0
  • Memorial Basketball Scholarship
  • Perfect State College Basketball Scholarship -3 yr letter award
  • Perfect State College Baseball Scholarship -3 yr letter award
  • Rotary Club-Susie Dingbat Scholarship
  • Academic Honors List
  • Varsity Club President
  • Phi Beta Landing Business Sorority

PERSONAL: Married, 1 child

Meet Pat Peoples. This résumé would not get to the top of the pile, and it may find the round file. Like Barb's original, Pat's was lacking accomplishments. It was overkill on bullet points, but they were not used to accentuate accomplishments. Using bullet points for everything dilutes their impact.

BEFORE

Pat Peoples
1700 N. Capital Blvd. ■ (Anyplace, TX 78746 ■ ((310) 706-0123) ■ patpeoples@always.com

OBJECTIVE

A challenging career in outside sales where I can utilize my extensive experience and skills in sales, marketing, communication, and networking to achieve the highest company, career, and personal goals.

SUMMARY

- Over ten years of successful sales experience with six years in solution selling (multimedia, print, e-commerce advertising, and search engine optimization and marketing services)
- Proven ability to increase sales and maximize profitability by:
  - Creating and implementing innovative sales strategies and customized product/service offerings and proposals
  - Consistently building a solid pipeline of qualified prospects by cold calling, cultivating leads and developing referrals
  - Establishing strong, long-term client and agency relationships through excellent customer service
  - Maintaining extensive product and market knowledge
- Adept at cold calling, prospecting, negotiating & closing business, and account management/ development
- Ability to manage existing operations through changes in technology, product repositioning, and various financial environments
- Effective leader, self-starter, problem-solver, and team player dedicated to exceeding goals
- Proficient in Microsoft Office (Word, Excel, PowerPoint, Outlook,) sales management software, and numerous software, hardware, and internet products/services
- Knowledge of online advertising technologies, including third party ad serving, rich media, and emerging ad-targeting and search technology

BEFORE

PROFESSIONAL EXPERIENCE

Perfectmix, Chicago, IL   2006 to present
(Performance-Based Marketing Division of Demonink)
Account Executive South West Region
- Develop and close deals with top brand marketers to sell their products/services via Perfectmix Paid Search Marketing, Search Engine Optimization, and Affiliate Marketing Services
- Work collaboratively and effectively with all levels of staff including senior management, marketing, and external strategic business partner contacts at Google and Yahoo! & top advertising agencies
- Construct customized presentations and proposals using competitive intelligence and marketing data from third party resources such as HitWise, AdGooRoo, Forrester, Yahoo! Buzz, & Comscore
- Present proprietary search technology and competitive advantages to Vice Presidents of Marketing of top retailers and companies such as CBS, Epson, Disney, Mazda, Countrywide, Guess, Toyota, etc.
- Accomplishments:
    ◦ Achieved quarterly business objectives and sales goals

Los Angeles Grind, Los Angeles, CA   1999 to 2006
Senior Account Executive
- Aggressively developed Southern California market for internet recruiting services, banner advertisements, and multi media campaigns for Fortune 500 and 1000 companies
- Launched Careerbuilder.com in So. California market in 1999; successfully grew Los Angeles Grind market share to become the #1 Tribune newspaper for Careerbuilder sales for five consecutive years
- Educated VP's, decision makers and agencies to emerging online technology and innovation while supporting the benefits and need for multimedia recruitment and branding strategies
- Repositioned competitive role against industry leaders such as Monster.com and HotJobs.com
- Trained, mentored, and motivated Recruitment Classifieds Division to drive sales by developing sales skills and online advertising product knowledge
- Most sales involve annual or semi-annual commitment. Client list includes Boeing, Mitsubishi, Healthnet, Northrop Grumman, Corinthian Colleges, Ameriquest
- Accomplishments and Awards:
    ◦ Achieved #1 Online Sales Person Classifieds Division 2004; 132% Quota 2005
    ◦ Exceeded yearly quota for 5 consecutive years by 128% to 165%
    ◦ Awarded Los Angeles Times 2001 Online Sales Person of the Year
    ◦ Earned #1 Sales Person CalendarLive 1999, 2000

GoodFood.com, San Francisco, CA   1997 to 1999
Regional Sales Representative
- Established new Southern California territory and collaborated in designing the sales strategy and training collateral that grew company sales force from 4 to 60 representatives nationwide
- Executed sales through effective cold calling, canvassing, lead generation, and referral programs
- Created and implemented regional sales and marketing strategies to consistently grow new customer base to 180 new customers first year
- Clients consisted of numerous restaurant chains including Dominos, Brinker International, Patina
- Accomplishments and Awards:
    ◦ Produced top sales in the region and 4th in the nation (out of 60 sales representatives) in 1998 generating 9.2% of the company's annual revenue

Equiscam International, Inc., Las Vegas, NV   1995 to 1997
Sales and Marketing Representative
- Conducted sales presentations, product trainings, and negotiated contracts with clients
- Serviced existing accounts which included restaurants, real estate developers, and other commercial businesses
- Established and expanded client database through cold calling and client referral programs
- Accomplishments:
    ◦ Achieved the ranking of the top 3 sales representative in the nation June 1996

BEFORE

EDUCATION

BS Psychology / Cum Laude Texas A&M University 1993
2001-2005 Careerbuilder.com Bi-annual Training Seminars
2000 Non-Manipulative Selling
1999 SPIN Selling
1993-1994 University of North Texas
       Masters Graduate Program

I'm also not a big fan of the "Objective" as I discussed earlier. They're usually too general (like Pat's) and don't really add anything. If an item on a résumé doesn't add anything, it detracts from your first impression. The proper "Objective" would be listing your ideal job by title, but it is not a needed item. My advice: Get rid of it and use the extra space for impactful accomplishments.

I also don't like the "Summary." It says, "I know you won't really read my résumé so I'll give you the same information twice." Lose the "Summary" and stick with the recommended format: list activities in sentence form, and then bullet-point your accomplishments in order of importance.

In addition, Pat's résumé was convoluted, bouncing around with accomplishments and responsibilities with no cohesiveness. It also employed passive words like executed, implemented, conducted, and serviced. If you are trying to paint yourself as a hard-charger and a winner, then passive words won't cut it. Not many employers say, "Get me someone who is a good implementer! A real executer. Someone who can conduct things and service an existing client."

My advice: use action words such as successfully sold, created, developed, obtained, ranked #1, earned, and launched.

Judge for yourself. Then we'll look at the makeover.

AFTER

Pat Peoples
1700 N. Capital Blvd. ■ (Anyplace, TX 78746 ■ ((310) 706-0123) ■ patpeoples@always.com

PROFESSIONAL EXPERIENCE

Perfectmix, Chicago, IL   2006 to present
(Performance-Based Marketing Division of Demonink)

Account Executive - Southwest Region

Responsible for Sales of Perfectmix Paid Search Marketing, Search Engine Optimization, and Affiliate Marketing Services targeting U.S. Companies. Primarily target C-Level executives at Fortune 500 Companies using competitive intelligence and marketing data from 3rd party resources such as: HitWise, AdGooRoo, Forrester, Yahoo!, Buzz, & Comscore.

- Increased revenue by 217%.
- Ranked #1 out of 14 Account Executives.
- Obtained new business with ABC Corporation accounting for $1.2 million in new revenue.
- ABC Corporation became Perfectmix's most profitable customer in year one.
- Obtained new business with 123 Incorporated worth an incremental $1.1 million.
- Won Circle of Excellence Trip Award.

Los Angeles Grind, Los Angeles, CA   1999 to 2006

Senior Account Executive

Responsible for the Southern California market for internet recruiting services, banner advertisements, and multi media campaigns for Fortune 500 and 1000 companies. Client target list includes Boeing, Mitsubishi, Healthnet, Northrop Grumman, Corinthian Colleges, and Ameriquest. Launched Careerbuilder.com in So. California market in 1999.

- Achieved #1 Online Sales Person out of 13 in the Classifieds Division 2004.
- Exceeded yearly quota for 5 consecutive years by 128% to 165%.
- Obtained a 132% increase versus Quota in 2005.
- Awarded Los Angeles Grind's 2001 Online Sales Person of the Year.
- Successfully increased Los Angeles Grind market share to become the #1 Tribune newspaper for Careerbuilder sales for five consecutive years.
- Ranked #1 Sales Person for CalendarLive in 1999, 2000.

GoodFood.com, San Francisco, CA   1997 to 1999

Regional Sales Representative

Responsible for United States Business Development targeting the Restaurant industry in a start-up environment. Designed the sales strategy and training collateral for new markets.

- Obtained 180 new customers in year one which led to an incremental $2 million in revenue, including Dominos, Brinker International, and Patina.
- Produced #1 sales in the Region and ranked #4 out of 60 nationally in 1998.
- Built company sales force from 4 to 60 Regional Sales Representatives through a 7 member multi-functional team effort.

AFTER

Pat Peoples — 2

Equiscam International, Inc., Las Vegas, NV   1995 to 1997

Sales and Marketing Representative

Primary responsibilities include managing the existing client base and developing new business in the Restaurant, Real Estate Developer, and other Commercial Businesses.

- Ranked #3 out of 57 Sales and Marketing Representatives in the nation in 1996.
- Obtained over $1.1 million in new business with Sysco Distributors, servicing TGI Fridays, and Benningtons.

ADDITIONAL TRAINING

Careerbuilder.com Bi-annual Training Seminars, 2001-2005
Non-Manipulative Selling, 2000
SPIN Selling, 1999

EDUCATION

University of North Texas
Masters Graduate Program (completed 30 credit hours)
GPA: 3.4/4.0

Texas A&M University
BS Psychology
Cum Laude Honors; GPA: 3.3/4.0

Did you see how we cleaned up Pat's résumé, making the accomplishments hard-hitting and meaningful? We consistently used strong action words in describing accomplishments. This résumé became much clearer and more concise. Pat was thrilled with the improvements. They took Pat less than a half-hour. The result: job offer and dream job!

NOTES:

Have you seen enough sample résumés yet? I hope the before and after examples were compelling and made you want to take another look at your résumé. I will end this important section with a practical template to use as you make over your own résumé. All you have to do is fill in the blanks. It really is easy to follow and takes away any of your résumé phobias:

Fill in your name: _____

Street Address: _____

City, State, Zip Code: _____

Cell phone number: _____

Professional Experience: _____

Most recent employer: _____

Month, Year of start – Present: _____

Current Job Title: _____

Month, Year – Present: _____

Describe what you do in three sentences (responsibility, scope, industry, points of relevance)
  - List greatest accomplishment
    (remember to quantify and qualify it)

_____

_____

- List second greatest accomplishment

  _____

  _____

- List third greatest accomplishment

  _____

  _____

- List fourth greatest accomplishment

  _____

  _____

- List fifth greatest accomplishment

  _____

  _____

**Next company (if different)
or next job title:** _____

Month, Year of start – Present: _____

Current Job Title: _____

Month, Year – Present: _____

Describe what you do in three sentences (responsibility, scope, industry, points of relevance)
- List greatest accomplishment
  (remember to quantify and qualify it)

  _____

  _____

- List second greatest accomplishment

  _____

  _____

- List third greatest accomplishment

  _____

  _____

**Next company (if different)
or next job title:** _____

Month, Year of start – Present: _____

Current Job Title: _____

Month, Year – Present: _____

Describe what you do in three sentences (responsibility, scope, industry, points of relevance)
- List greatest accomplishment
  (remember to quantify and qualify it)

  _____

  _____

- List second greatest accomplishment

  _____

  _____

- List third greatest accomplishment

  _____

  _____

**Next company (if different)
or next job title:** _____

Month, Year of start – Present: _____

Current Job Title: _____

Month, Year – Present: _____

Describe what you do in three sentences (responsibility, scope, industry, points of relevance)

- List greatest accomplishment
  (remember to quantify and qualify it)

  _____

  _____

- List second greatest accomplishment

  _____

  _____

- List third greatest accomplishment

  _____

  _____

And so on for the companies you have worked for and various positions you have held.

Additional Training

- List most impressive applicable training you have received by title and date _____

  _____

- List second most impressive applicable training you have received by title and date _____

  _____

- List third most impressive applicable training you have received by title and date _____

  _____

- List fourth most impressive applicable training you have received by title and date _____

  _____

- List fifth most impressive applicable training you have received by title and date_____

  _____

Education

- College or University Name _____

- Year started – year finished if 4 years; if not, list year finished

- Degree_____

- GPA (if over a 3.0 out of 4.0 scale, list it; if not, they assume you have the John Belushi GPA) _____

- Honors (Magna, Summa, or Cum Laude if it applies to you)

Financed percentage of education costs through part-time work—list if over 50%.

Personal

Married, number of children is desirable; if thrice divorced and living in a van down by the river, skip it!

Congratulations—you've just written your résumé. Now, sleep on it, let your subconscious take over, and see how it improves over the next few days. You'll probably be able to tighten up your descriptions and may come up with some new accomplishments or at least quantify and qualify them better. Compare this first draft with your finished product—your final should be a killer résumé.

NOTES:

Your Killer Résumé, Second Draft

Most recent employer: _____

Month, Year of start – Present: _____

Current Job Title: _____

Month, Year – Present: _____

Describe what you do in three sentences (responsibility, scope, industry, points of relevance)

- List greatest accomplishment
  (remember to quantify and qualify it)

  _____

  _____

- List second greatest accomplishment

  _____

  _____

- List third greatest accomplishment

  _____

  _____

- List fourth greatest accomplishment

  _____

  _____

- List fifth greatest accomplishment

  _____

  _____

Next company (if different)
or next job title: _____

Month, Year of start – Present: _____

Current Job Title: _____

Month, Year – Present: _____

Describe what you do in three sentences (responsibility, scope, industry, points of relevance)

- List greatest accomplishment
  (remember to quantify and qualify it)

  _____

  _____

- List second greatest accomplishment

  _____

  _____

- List third greatest accomplishment

  _____

  _____

**Next company (if different)
or next job title:** _____

Month, Year of start – Present: _____

Current Job Title: _____

Month, Year – Present: _____

Describe what you do in three sentences (responsibility, scope, industry, points of relevance)

- List greatest accomplishment
  (remember to quantify and qualify it)

_____

_____

- List second greatest accomplishment

_____

_____

- List third greatest accomplishment

_____

_____

Next company (if different)
or next job title: _____

Month, Year of start – Present: _____

Current Job Title: _____

Month, Year – Present: _____

Describe what you do in three sentences (responsibility, scope, industry, points of relevance)

- List greatest accomplishment
  (remember to quantify and qualify it)

  _____

  _____

- List second greatest accomplishment

  _____

  _____

- List third greatest accomplishment

  _____

  _____

**Next company (if different)
or next job title:** _____

Month, Year of start – Present: _____

Current Job Title: _____

Month, Year – Present: _____

Describe what you do in three sentences (responsibility, scope, industry, points of relevance)

- List greatest accomplishment
  (remember to quantify and qualify it)

  _____

  _____

- List second greatest accomplishment

  _____

  _____

- List third greatest accomplishment

  _____

  _____

Additional Training

- List most impressive applicable training you have received by title and date _____
  _____

- List second most impressive applicable training you have received by title and date _____
  _____

- List third most impressive applicable training you have received by title and date _____
  _____

- List fourth most impressive applicable training you have received by title and date _____
  _____

- List fifth most impressive applicable training you have received by title and date _____
  _____

Education

- College or University Name ....

- Year started – year finished if 4 years; if not, list year finished

- Degree..

- GPA (if over a 3.0 out of 4.0 scale, list it; if not, they assume you have the John Belushi GPA) ....

- Honors (Magna, Summa, or Cum Laude if it applies to you)

Financed percentage of education costs through part-time work—list if over 50%.

Personal

Review and repeat your drafts using this model until you have a clean, impressive representation of who you are and what you can bring to the table.

NOTES:

Your Bliss List
Journal

Your Bliss List Journal

Need more room to express your thoughts? You can do it right here! Write to your heart's content, and then some. Feel free to just pick a topic and go with it – you never know where you might end up or what you'll discover about yourself.

Your Bliss Cards

Your Bliss Cards

I t's a good idea to write your Top Seven Bliss List items on a card, and carry it with you. There are blank 3-x-5 cards available for you to cut out on the following pages. Make sure to keep your Bliss Cards in a strategic place where you are most apt to view them often during the day.

Do:

- put a date on your Bliss Card
- write your goal as if it has already happened
- be detailed on your Bliss Cards
- use measurable goals

Do not:

- use "I wish", "I hope", "I think"
- use negative or vengeful language

After you have achieved one of the items on your Bliss List, make a new one and save your card in a folder labeled "Bliss List Successes."

March 31

I'm enjoying my new job this summer!
Great pay, smart people, challenging work, long-term
potential.

Your Bliss Jar

Your Bliss Jar

ake a jar and tape a note on top of the jar stating, "Whatever is contained in this Bliss Jar—IS!" Write each goal individually on a small piece of paper, then reread it with enthusiastic feeling, and simply drop each one into the jar. You will be amazed at how many of your little notes actually come true.

To get started, you may want to use the fifteen items you listed in your original *Bliss List*. Though you pared the list down to seven so you wouldn't overload your brain, capable of handling only seven things at once, you cannot overload your Bliss Jar. There are no limits. Write all fifteen goals down separately and drop 'em into the jar. It will start working its magic right after you close the lid on the jar.

June 1

I landed 3 new clients this year!

To get full use out of *The Bliss List Journal*, it's best to first read *The Bliss List: The Ultimate Guide to Living the Dream at Work and Beyond!* Learn how to attract bliss into your life, by changing your attitude and your mind. *The Bliss List* will provide you with insight and inspiration to find work that truly brings you bliss.

Available online at www.YourBlissList.com!